WORLD'S SMALLEST DINOSAURS

Rupert Matthews

www.raintreepublishers.co.uk
Visit our website to find out
more information about
Raintree books.

To order:
☎ Phone 0845 6044371
🖨 Fax +44 (0) 1865 312263
💻 Email myorders@raintreepublishers.co.uk

Customers from outside the UK please telephone +44 1865 312262

Raintree is an imprint of **Capstone Global Library Limited**,
a company incorporated in England and Wales having its
registered office at 7 Pilgrim Street, London, EC4V 6LB –
Registered company number: 6695582

Edited by Rebecca Rissman and Laura Knowles
Designed by Richard Parker
Picture research by Mica Brancic
Originated by Capstone Global Library Ltd
Printed and bound in China by CTPS

ISBN 978 1 4062 3465 7
15 14 13 12 11
10 9 8 7 6 5 4 3 2 1

British Library Cataloguing in Publication Data
Matthews, Rupert.
World's smallest dinosaurs. -- (Extreme dinosaurs)
567.9-dc22
A full catalogue record for this book is available from
the British Library.

Acknowledgements
We would like to thank the following for permission to
reproduce images: © Capstone Publishers pp. 4 (James Field),
5 (James Field), 7 (James Field), 9 (James Field), 8 (Steve
Weston), 11 (Steve Weston), 10 (James Field), 13 (Steve
Weston), 12 (James Field), 14 (Steve Weston), 15 (Steve
Weston), 16 (James Field), 17 (James Field), 18 (James Field),
19 (James Field), 20 (James Field), 21 (Steve Weston), 23
(Steve Weston), 22 (Steve Weston), 24 (James Field), 25 (Steve
Weston), 27 (James Field), 26 (James Field); Shutterstock p. 29
(© Geoff Hardy).

Background design features reproduced with permission of
Shutterstock/© Szefei/© Fedorov Oleksiy/© Oleg Golovnev/
© Nuttakit.

Cover image of a *Sinosauropteryx* reproduced with permission
of © Capstone Publishers/James Field.

We would like to thank Nathan Smith for his invaluable help in
the preparation of this book.

Every effort has been made to contact copyright holders of
material reproduced in this book. Any omissions will be
rectified in subsequent printings if notice is given to the
publishers.

Contents

Some words are shown in bold, **like this**.
You can find out what they mean by
looking in the glossary.

The littlest dinosaurs

Dinosaurs were a group of animals that lived millions of years ago. Some dinosaurs were the biggest animals ever to walk the Earth. But others were as small as a chicken! There were tiny dinosaurs of all kinds. There were small hunters, small plant-eaters, and small **scavengers**. Some dinosaurs were so small that they ate insects.

Four-winged flyer

Microraptor was about 60 centimetres long. That is about as long as a small dog. It probably hunted insects, worms, and other small animals.

Microraptor had short feathers on its body and long wing feathers. It looked a bit like a turkey! The feathers helped to keep it warm.

Did you know?
Microraptor could glide
a long distance if it leapt
from a high place.

The armoured pygmy

Ankylosaurian dinosaurs were heavy animals that were as big as tanks and covered in bone **armour**. But *Minmi* was only about 3 metres long – about the size of a horse. Large plates of bone with sharp points grew from its tail. If it was attacked by hunting dinosaurs it would have swung its tail at them to drive them away.

"Compy"

The hunting **dinosaur** *Compsognathus* was about the size of a small turkey. It caught lizards, mammals, and bugs with its hands. Each hand was smaller than your thumb. It lived beside the sea where there were shallow **lagoons** and wide beaches. Its long legs and powerful muscles meant it could move quickly when hunting for food.

Did you know?
Compsognathus is called "Compy" in the film **Jurassic** Park. No scientist ever uses this name.

Compsognathus

Tiny hunters

The European **dinosaur** *Saltopus* was about the size of a small cat. It had hollow bones and weighed about 7 kilograms. It walked on its back legs. The long, thin jaws contained dozens of small, sharp teeth. *Timimus* was a similar dinosaur that lived in Australia. The leg bones of *Timimus* are among the thinnest of all dinosaur bones.

Timimus

Saltopus

13

On the plains

Lesothosaurus was a plant-eating **dinosaur** that lived on hot, dry plains in southern Africa. It was less than one metre long. That's about the same size as a dog. It had long legs so that it could run quickly to escape danger. When it stood upright it still would not have reached your knee.

Lesothosaurus

Did you know?

Atlascopcosaurus was a similar dinosaur from Australia. The place where **fossils** of *Atlascopcosaurus* were found has been renamed "Dinosaur Cove".

Little boneheads

The **dinosaur** with the longest name was *Micropachycephalosaurus*, but it was one of the smallest dinosaurs. It was about half a metre long. It had thick bone on top of its head. This may have been used to headbutt rivals in fights.

Scutellosaurus had bone plates along its back and on its head. Both these dinosaurs were plant-eaters that could walk on their back feet or on all fours.

Micropachycephalosaurus

Scutellosaurus

Colourful hunter

The Asian **dinosaur** *Sinosauropteryx* was about one metre long. Most of that length was the long, thin tail. It was covered in small feathers that would have helped keep it warm. **Fossils** of the dinosaur's feathers show that *Sinosauropteryx* had dark stripes on its body and tail. The back of the animal was probably yellowish or reddish in colour.

Bambiraptor

The hunting **dinosaur** *Bambiraptor* stood about 30 centimetres tall. Even if it stretched, it would not have been able to reach much higher than your knee! Its front legs ended in three strong claws that it used to grab **prey**. *Bambiraptor* belonged to a group of raptors who had bigger brains than some other dinosaurs, so it was possibly cleverer than other dinosaurs.

Shield faces

Ceratopsian dinosaurs are famous for having long horns on their heads and bone shields over their necks. Strong muscles connected to the shield worked the jaws. However, the smallest ceratopsians had no horns at all. *Graciliceratops* was about a metre long. *Protoceratops* was the size of a pony. It walked on all four legs and had a neck shield.

Protoceratops

Did you know?
Graciliceratops walked on its hind feet.

neck shield

Graciliceratops

Special teeth

Some small **dinosaurs** had special teeth for eating certain foods. *Incisivosaurus* was only one metre long, about the length of a labrador dog. It had long teeth in the front of its mouth. It may have used these teeth to reach seeds in pine cones or to get at other seeds or nuts. *Archaeoceratops* had a narrow beak. This may have been used to nip leaves off palms or ferns.

Incisivosaurus

Archaeoceratops

Leaping for insects

Protarchaeopteryx was up to 2 metres long. Its body was about the size of a large goose. It had long feathers on its arms and on its tail. Some scientists think that it could leap into the air to catch flying insects. The feathers may have helped it stay in the air. Others think it ran about catching food on the ground. The feathers might have been used to display to other **dinosaurs**.

Protarchaeopteryx

How to become a museum curator

A museum curator is the person who is in charge of museum collections. The curator decides what objects should be on display and when the museum will be open. Most curators have been to university. They will then have done **research** work about a particular subject. They might have looked into the **Mesozoic Era**, also known as the "Age of **Dinosaurs**". They will probably have worked at the museum, showing people around and explaining the display to visitors.

Glossary

ankylosaurians family of armoured plant-eating dinosaurs that lived between 160 and 65 million years ago

armour outer shell or bone on some dinosaurs that protected their bodies

ceratopsian family of horned plant-eating dinosaurs that lived in North America and Asia towards the end of the Age of Dinosaurs

dinosaur group of animals that lived on land millions of years ago during the Mesozoic Era

fossil part of a plant or animal that has been buried in rocks for millions of years

Jurassic part of Earth's history that began about 200 million years ago and ended about 145 million years ago

lagoon shallow body of salt water near the sea, surrounded by sandbanks

Mesozoic Era part of Earth's history that is sometimes called the "Age of Dinosaurs". It is divided into three periods: Triassic, Jurassic, and Cretaceous.

prey animal that is killed by another for food

research study of a particular subject such as dinosaurs

scavengers animals that feed on dead animals

Find out more

Books

Dinosaur Encyclopedia, Caroline Bingham
(Dorling Kindersley, 2009)
Dinosaurs, Stephanie Turnbull (Usborne, 2006)
First Encyclopedia of Dinosaurs and Prehistoric Life,
Sam Taplin (Usborne, 2011)
Who Cleans Dinosaur Bones?: Working at a Museum,
(Wild Work) Margie Markarian (Raintree, 2010)

Websites

www.dinosaurden.co.uk
Information about dinosaurs, as well as puzzles and games can
be found on this site.

www.nhm.ac.uk/kids-only/dinosaurs
The Natural History Museum's website has lots of information
about dinosaurs, including facts, quizzes, and games.

www.thedinosaurmuseum.com/html/dinosaur-facts.html
Find out more about dinosaurs on the Dinosaur Museum website.

Index